Credits

Setting	A Real life event on the St Lawrence River, with a swan during Winter of 2018-2019
Story and Layout	Rodney and Lieselotte Bartlett
Photos	Bartletts
Production	2020 Ingram Spark
Font	Baskerville Old Face
Version 2.3	April 2021
ISBN	978-0-9937856-6-5 April 22, 2020
Copyright	Rodney and Lieselotte Bartlett
	All rights reserved

One Hungry Swan

An old couple stood at the banks of the St. Lawrence River outside their home. They had watched for days, as flocks of Canada Geese and Snow Geese took off to the lands of the South, with a cacophony of calls and rushing sounds of beating wings.

The Ospreys too, who had been fishing right there all summer long, had left. The little mink they had often seen scurrying along the river's edge was no longer active and had begun his long winter sleep under the roots of the old Willow tree.

It was past Christmas now. Quiet and cold had settled on the land.

The river froze here and the river froze there. Ice was all around. Shards piled up in heaps with glass breaking sound. Opa and Oma, as the grandchildren called the old couple, bundled up and walked along the freezing river. Towards the bay a stubborn spot of water remained open where the current runs strong.

"Look!" said Oma, "there is a Snow goose left out there." "No, it can't be! It is too big," said Opa. "It is a swan! Also, there is little black duck keeping him company!"

"Oh my, this is the first time we've seen a swan here." Both stopped and peered into the cold. Sure enough; there was a swan swimming in the open lead. They admired the bird a while longer and then headed back home to their warm house.

No matter how cold, day after day the old people walked and watched for the unlikely pair in the river. Every day they saw the intrepid swan and his companion feeding. But their water hole was shrinking, getting smaller and smaller. "They better get out of there before it is too late!" said Opa. The little black duck must have heard him, for the next day he was gone.

But the majestic swan was still there, feeding and floating gracefully. Why did he not leave as well?

Was he a loner? Was he injured? Was he too weak?

Checking on the feeding spot a few days later, Swannie, as they now called him, was nowhere to be seen. "He finally got the message! I guess we won't see that silly old bird again", said Oma with a sigh. "Maybe you are right!" Opa agreed. They both had liked seeing that tough swan out there and would miss him.

Next morning Oma looked out the window:

"Come quickly! Look who is coming up the driveway!!"

Opa hurried to join her and both exclaimed, "Swannie is coming into our yard!" and watched him waddle toward the house.

But, something was not quite right.

Swannie took a few steps.   Then he sat down to rest.   He walked a little further and rested again.

"He can hardly walk, and look, he's caked in mud!"

"He seems exhausted! I bet he is hungry, the poor thing! Let's see if he will eat!" Oma said.

Quickly they gathered a few greens and some birdseed. Opa bundled up and walked down the driveway toward the swan. The swan got up and waddled towards Opa.

He was hungry alright.

He gobbled up all the old man gave him.

Oma brought a bowl of warm water. Swannie loved dipping his long beak into the water and taking long slurps. Then he lifted his head to the sky. Was it to let the water run down inside his long neck? The Swan did this over and over, drinking and drinking until the bowl was empty.

Content now, he tucked his head under his wing and promptly took a nap right there beside the house.

Opa and Oma kept an eye on him. Looking out later, they saw him waddling painfully, slowly back to the river.

Day after day the old couple fed the ailing swan. As soon as he saw Opa coming with the feed, Swannie waddled up from the river and headed straight to the feeding spot.

One day Opa went out to check on Swannie. He found him sitting in the middle of the road.

"Come on Buddy, you can't stay here, you might get killed. Come on now, you need to get off the road, a snow plow may come along soon." Hearing the sound of rattling corn treats, the swan gathered up his strength and was lured away from the road toward safety.

At dusk, returning from their walk, they turned into their driveway. They were startled, as a fox, equally startled, shot right passed them, racing up the snow-bank and down toward the river, with his red tail straight out. "Oh no! Let's hope Swannie sees him coming!"

It was getting too dark now to watch the drama or to help their friend. There was nothing for them to do but go home and have their supper. But they were worried for him.

First thing next morning they looked out the window. Wind was howling, snow was drifting here and snow was piling up there. Where was Swannie in that bitter cold? Did the foxes finally get him? Did he lie under a pile of snow by the river's edge? They walked out into the snow storm to look for him, but there was not a white feather to be seen in the white-out of the storm. Disappointed they returned home.

That evening, they stood by the window next to the woodstove. A cheery fire cast a warm glow into the room, dispelling their gloom. The light from the house shone invitingly through the window into the black night.

Peering out into the dark Oma exclaimed, "What is that big lump out there? Could that be Swannie?" Both were glued to the window now. Sure enough! On the wind-sheltered side of the house in a shaft of light, the swan sat with his head buried deep under his wing. They were so excited to see him and talked rather loudly. The Swan heard the excitement. Out popped his head and he looked straight at them as if to say: "What did you expect?"

Oma slipped on her moccasins and quickly brought Swannie some supper and a whole bucket of warm water. Running back inside, they watched him hungrily devour his meal . This time he stuck his whole head into the bucket and dabbled on the bottom, occasionally coming up for air. How he loved that warm water! He preened himself and he cleaned himself. He looked at them standing by the window seeming to say: "Thank you. And Good Night!" Once more he tucked his head under his wing and went off to sleep.

Oma got up at 3 in the morning and of course she had to check on that silly old bird, but he was gone! "I don't know *what he* does this time of night, but I have confidence in him. He is a proven survivor!"

And so he was. Day after day he waddled up to their house to come for his meal. One day he managed to hop right up the steps of the front porch. When Oma opened the door, Swannie quickly thrust his long neck into the opening trying to come into the warm house. BUT that's where Oma drew the line. "No! You are NOT coming into the house! You stay outside where you belong."

Swannie's fame spread over the neighbourhood. Neighbours would stop Oma and Opa on the road and say: "How is Swannie doing today?" Others would come up the driveway and say: "Here is some more feed for your pet." He even got his picture in the newspaper.

Finally a warm wind from the South began to blow. The river nibbled and gnawed at the edge of the ice, cracking and piling, smoothing and filing, loosening pieces to float down stream. Released from its icy prison, the river was opening up more and more.

Swannie gained enough strength and had returned to his feeding spot. One day, Oma and Opa walked down the river's edge. "How is it going out there Swannie buddy? I suppose you don't need any more food from us now, do you?" Opa called out to him.

At this the Swan swam rapidly toward him. "We better get out of here," Oma coached. "We didn't bring anything to feed him." With his long neck straining forward, he seemed determined to reach the old man. "Never you mind coming for corn, just go back to eating your seaweed."

The Swan, seeing that he could not keep up with the old folks on land, obeyed and went back to feeding in the river. And it was good thing the did.

For just then, they heard the loud swish, swishing sound of beating wings. Looking up they thrilled to see three more swans. Now with their enormous wings set, they glided barely above their heads and landed gracefully next to Swannie, the Survivor. "Hah, they don't honk any greetings!" "No, they don't honk. I guess that is why they are called Mute Swans instead of Trumpters. But look how beautiful they are, truly some of God's majestic creatures!" admired Opa.

What a picture they made! The graceful birds swam along the edge of the ice floating down the now open path of the river, just in front of the old couple's house. "It looks like two of them are really taking to each other", they chuckled. One fluffed up his plumage looking much bigger now and swam circles around his lady.

What a sight! "Which one do you think is Swannie?" they asked each other. "Hm, hard to say, we may never know for sure."

Romance was definitely in the air.

The two swans put their heads together, their long necks forming the shape of a heart, gliding around each other in a mesmerizing dance. What a pair they were!

Suddenly, all four swans spread their powerful wings and with one accord lifted out of the water. They winged their way downriver under the pewter afternoon sky and were gone.

The old folks sometimes look wistfully out the window, wondering if they might see Swannie waddling up to the house once again. Was he really gone for good? On their walks along the river they kept an eye out for him.

"Look" said Oma, while on a spring walk, "there's a pair of swans". Heading down the riverbank for a closer look, they called out "Swaaaannie!" but sadly, there was no familiar response. Upon a closer look they saw the black beaks of tundra swans. For sure this was not their Swannie.

"Oh well!" Opa mused "It was a nice thought! Hm, coming to think of it, I wonder why that bird chose our home for a handout in the first place?" "Oh I don't know, he probably thought we were a couple of old softies, but I am sure glad he did."